I0815371

HISTORY OF HOLIDAYS AND FESTIVALS

ROSH HASHANAH

BY HILARY MARGITICH

CONTENT CONSULTANT
Samuel J. Kessler, PhD
Assistant Professor of Religion
Gustavus Adolphus College

Cover image: On Rosh Hashanah, some Jews pray at holy sites, such as the graves of important rabbis.

An Imprint of Abdo Publishing
abdobooks.com

abdobooks.com

Printed in the United States of America, North Mankato, Minnesota.
102023
012024

Cover Photo: Oleksandr Rupeta/NurPhoto/Getty Images
Interior Photos: Erez Lichtfeld/Sipa/AP Images, 4–5, 45; Jupiter Images/The Image Bank/Getty Images, 6; Red Line Editorial, 8, 15; Al Seib/Los Angeles Times/Getty Images, 9; Michael Jacobs/Art in All of Us/Corbis News/Getty Images, 12–13; iStockphoto, 14, 16, 43; Artokoloro/Penta Springs Limited/Alamy, 18; Yehoshua Halevi/iStockphoto, 20–21; Painters/Alamy, 23; Shutterstock Images, 24, 38; Debbie Hill/UPI/Alamy, 28–29; Nataly Hanin/iStockphoto, 30; Oleksandr Rupeta/Alamy, 34–35; Emmanuel Dunand/AFP/Getty Images, 36; Jason Armond/Los Angeles Times/Getty Images, 40

Editor: Laura Stickney
Series Designer: Ryan Gale

Library of Congress Control Number: 2023939661

Publisher's Cataloging-in-Publication Data
Names: Margitich, Hilary, author.
Title: Rosh Hashanah / by Hilary Margitich
Description: Minneapolis, Minnesota: Abdo Publishing, 2024 | Series: History of holidays and festivals | Includes online resources and index.
Identifiers: ISBN 9781098292645 (lib. bdg.) | ISBN 9798384910589 (ebook)
Subjects: LCSH: Holidays--Juvenile literature. | Fasts and feasts--Juvenile literature. | Rosh ha-Shanah--Juvenile literature. | Jewish New Year--Juvenile literature. | Judaism--Customs and practices--Juvenile literature. | High Holidays--Juvenile literature.
Classification: DDC 296.431--dc23

CONTENTS

CHAPTER ONE

WELCOMING A NEW YEAR

It's early autumn in the United States. A steady stream of people files into a Jewish synagogue for the morning Rosh Hashanah service. Many people wear new clothing for this occasion. Some wear all white. The people fill every seat in the synagogue. They have all come to honor God as their king.

During the service, the people listen to a cantor sing prayers. Then they recite the prayers back from a special prayer book. The rabbi reads sections from the Torah, the first

A traditional shofar is usually made from a hollowed ram's horn. Some shofars are large and spiral shaped, while others are much smaller.

Dipping apples in honey has been a Rosh Hashanah tradition for centuries. Apples are believed to be a symbolic fruit and are mentioned in several religious texts.

five books of the Hebrew Bible. Torahs are written on scrolls of parchment, a paper made from animal skins. Then everyone waits for the cry of the shofar, or ram's horn. Its trumpetlike sound echoes through the synagogue. It ushers in a new year, full of possibility. It is a time for Jewish people to look back on the past year and consider anything they said or did that hurt others. It is a time for personal reflection and prayers to God.

After the service, family and friends gather at home for celebratory meals. They eat apples, honey, and other symbolic foods. It is the start of the Days of Awe, a ten-day period of prayer and reflection. This is one of the most important times of the year for Jewish people.

STARTING AT SUNDOWN

All Jewish days, including holidays such as Rosh Hashanah, begin in the evening and continue until the following evening. This is because in Judaism, a new day begins at sunset rather than midnight. In the first book of the Torah, it says, "And there was evening, and there was morning, one day." It says this for all seven days of the week. Jews interpret this as meaning that a day begins at sunset. So evening is when they begin their worship and festivities.

JUDAISM AND ROSH HASHANAH

Judaism is the religion practiced by the Jewish people. It began in Israel, which is located in the Middle East. There, a small tribe of people called Jews stopped praying to many gods and started praying to just one God. Jews believe that they have a special relationship with God. Today, more than 15.2 million Jews live around the world. Some are ethnically Jewish but not religiously Jewish.

JUDAISM AROUND

THE WORLD

In 2021, the worldwide Jewish population was more than 15 million. This map shows the countries with the top ten highest Jewish populations. Why do you think there are more Jewish people living in these areas?

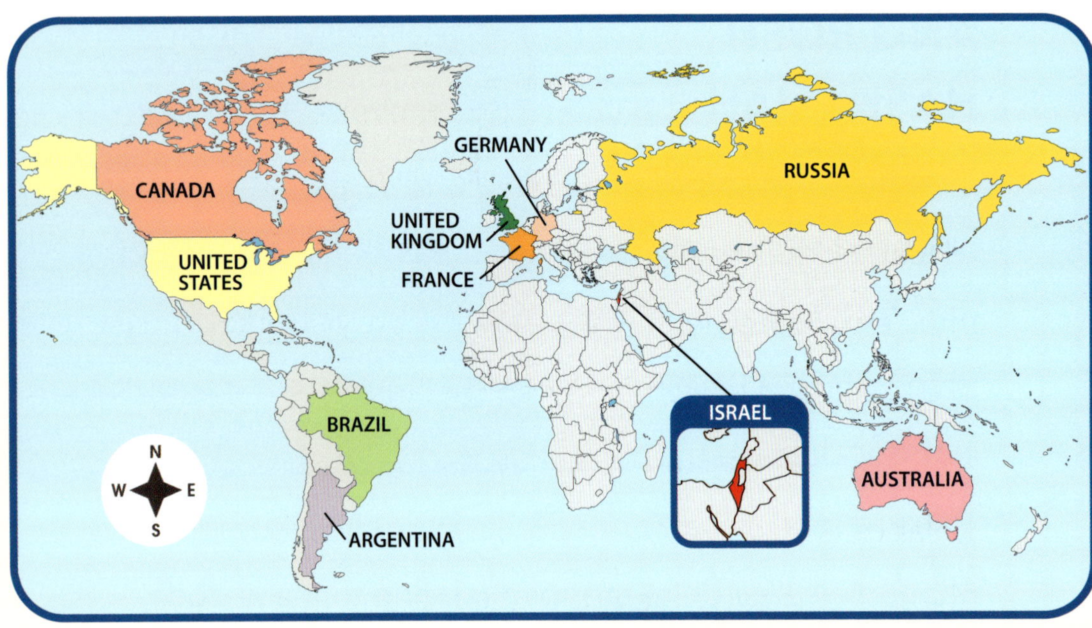

Israel	6,870,900		Argentina	175,000
United States	6,000,000		Russia	150,000
France	446,000		Germany	118,000
Canada	393,500		Australia	118,000
United Kingdom	292,000		Brazil	91,500

During Rosh Hashanah services, it is traditional to wear white. Some men wear caps called kippahs or yarmulkes. Those over age 13 may also wear a tallit, or prayer shawl.

Jews celebrate several major holidays during the year, including Rosh Hashanah. Rosh Hashanah means "Head of the Year" in Hebrew, the ancient language of the Jewish people. It is the Jewish new year and marks the day on which God created the universe.

The main calendar used in the western world is a solar calendar. It is based on Earth's movement around the sun. Each year begins in the month of January. But the Jewish calendar is both lunar and solar. It is based on the moon cycles and the cycle of seasons. Jews start counting a new year in Tishri, the seventh month. Tishri falls during September or early October.

PERSPECTIVES

TESHUVAH

To perform teshuvah, a person must pray to God for forgiveness for his or her sins. In other religions, prayer and repentance are often enough. But Jews believe that if a person has hurt someone, he or she also needs to apologize to that person and ask for forgiveness. According to Jewish tradition, one should ask a person for forgiveness at least three times. This gives the other person a chance to decide if he or she can forgive the person. The final step in teshuvah is changing one's future behavior so that the mistake is not repeated.

Rosh Hashanah starts at sundown on the first day of Tishri. The ten days that follow are called the Days of Awe or High Holidays. These days end with Yom Kippur. During this time, Jews take part in *teshuvah*, the process of seeking forgiveness.

Rosh Hashanah was not always a New Year celebration, although it has always been a major celebration for the Jewish people. Historical events and cultural influences helped shape the holiday over thousands of years. Its traditions and rituals continue to evolve.

STRAIGHT TO THE SOURCE

The shofar is an important part of Rosh Hashanah. Saadia Gaon was a Jewish scholar and philosopher who lived during the 900s CE. In his famous writings, Saadia tells the Jewish people why God commands them to blow the shofar during Rosh Hashanah:

> *This day is the beginning of creation when God created the world and ruled over it. At the beginning of a king's reign, they sound the trumpets and shofars, to [announce] in all locations that the new reign has begun; likewise, we accept upon ourselves God's reign on this day. . . .*
>
> *[Rosh Hashanah] is the 1st of the 10 Days of Teshuva, and we blow the shofar in order to announce that all those who wish to do teshuva, should do so!*

Source: Shaul Wertheimer. "Shofar: 11 Reasons Why." *Sefaria*, 29 Aug. 2018, sefaria.org. Accessed 7 Mar. 2023.

CONSIDER YOUR AUDIENCE

Adapt this passage for a different audience, such as a non-Jewish person. Write a blog post conveying this same information for the new audience. How does your post differ from the original text and why?

אין כניסה

CHAPTER TWO

THE ORIGINS OF ROSH HASHANAH

The book of Leviticus in the Hebrew Bible contains the first recorded account of Rosh Hashanah. The holiday is described as the first day of Tishri, set aside as a holy day of rest. It is a day for blowing the shofar and sacrificing animals. Jews sacrificed animals to show their dedication to God. They often did this at the Holy Temple in Jerusalem. Jerusalem is the ancient capital of the Jewish people, located in Israel. It was the site of two Holy Temples.

Today Jerusalem is a modern city. But the Old City area of Jerusalem is home to many important historical and religious sites, such as the Western Wall.

The first Holy Temple was also called Solomon's Temple, since it was built during King Solomon's reign. Historians don't know exactly what the temple looked like, but biblical texts describe it as a grand, highly decorated building.

The Hebrew prophet Ezekiel first used the name Rosh Hashanah in his writings, which date from around 592 BCE to 570 BCE. He used it to name the beginning of the year, when people cleansed the Temple of sin by sprinkling a young ox's blood. It later became the day on which the new year begins in the Jewish calendar.

BABYLONIAN CAPTIVITY

Babylonian Empire

This map shows Jerusalem and Babylon, the ancient capital of Babylonia where Jews were forced into exile. What can you tell about the span of the Babylonian Empire? What effects do you think this had on Jewish religion and ways of life?

BABYLONIAN INFLUENCE

Beginning in 597 BCE, people from Babylonia invaded the ancient Jewish kingdom of Judah. This kingdom included Jerusalem. The Babylonians destroyed the Temple. They forced the Jewish people to leave

When Ezra the Scribe returned to Jerusalem, he discovered that people in the city had not been following religious laws. To fix this, he read the Torah out loud to the Jewish people.

their homeland and remain in exile in Babylonia. Babylonia was located in what is now Iraq. In 539 BCE, Persia conquered Babylonia. Many of the Jewish people returned to their homeland the following year. They built the Second Temple several decades later.

According to the Hebrew Bible, Ezra the Scribe returned to Jerusalem in 458 BCE. He reorganized Jewish religious life. He held a convention on Rosh Hashanah. Ezra read from the Torah and told the Jews that they had strayed from God and must return to him. He said the day was sacred and joyful. They should celebrate it with rich food and sweet drinks.

Jews developed new religious practices after returning to Israel. Many were influenced by the Babylonian culture in which they had lived for many years. They began to use Babylonian names for months. Tishri, for example, is an ancient Babylonian word for "beginning." The Babylonians celebrated the new year with a festival in which they honored their gods, whom they believed prepared the world for the coming year. Jews adopted the practice

PERSPECTIVES

MONOTHEISM VS. POLYTHEISM

Judaism is a monotheistic religion, meaning Jews believe in one God. Christianity and Islam are also monotheistic. People who practice polytheistic religions, such as Hinduism, believe in many gods. The ancient Babylonians practiced polytheism. They celebrated and promised to serve their gods during an annual festival. This celebration likely formed the basis of what Rosh Hashanah became for the Jews. But Jewish religious leaders discouraged polytheistic celebrations. They emphasized God as the one true ruler.

The Roman invasion of Jerusalem was part of the First Jewish-Roman War (66–73 CE). Roman soldiers destroyed large portions of the city, setting the Second Temple on fire. Many Jewish people were killed or captured.

of celebrating the new year. Babylonians also observed a Day of Judgment during the festival, on which they believed their gods would judge every human. Each person's fate would be written on a tablet of destiny. This is believed to have evolved into Rosh Hashanah's theme of God judging every Jew.

TEMPLE DESTRUCTION

In 70 CE, the Romans destroyed the Second Temple. They ruled Jerusalem at the time. This final destruction of the Temple changed how Jews celebrated holidays. Sacrificing animals at the Temple had been the main focus of Jewish holidays. Without a Temple for performing sacrifices, Jews started focusing more on prayers and rituals at home and in synagogues. Different branches of Judaism developed their own traditions.

Over time, Jews showed flexibility in dealing with changing circumstances. This helped Judaism thrive throughout the world. The religion was able to survive many attempts to destroy it.

TEMPLE MOUNT

The Temple Mount in Jerusalem was the site of both the First and Second Temples. The Western Wall is the last surviving piece of the Second Temple. It stands just below the Mount. Jews from all over the world visit to see and pray by the wall. The Temple Mount is a very holy site for Jews, Christians, and Muslims. People of different faiths often gather at the site. This has sometimes caused tension and even violence. Today, the Mount is home to the Al-Aqsa Mosque and the Dome of the Rock, where Muslims believe the prophet Muhammed ascended to heaven.

מי שהיה נשוי פרק עשירי כתובות צה.
כתובות פרק עשירי מי שהיה נשוי

CHAPTER THREE

EARLY HISTORY

After returning to Israel from Babylonia, Jews began recognizing Rosh Hashanah as the new year and as a celebration of God's rule. Around 200 CE, rabbis wrote about the holiday. In their writings, they stressed the importance of the holiday and its themes. These themes shaped many of the holiday's rituals and practices. Over time, Rosh Hashanah practices became more widely celebrated among Jewish people.

The Talmud focuses on different aspects of Jewish religious law. Today, many Jewish people spend time studying the Talmud's writings.

THEMES AND RITUALS

After the destruction of the Second Temple, rabbis began writing more about celebrating Rosh Hashanah. Rabbis mention the holiday in the Mishnah. The Mishnah is a collection of rabbinic writings completed in about 220 CE. It is part of an important Jewish text called the Talmud, which includes writings from between 200 CE and 600 CE. According to the Mishnah, the world was created on the first day of Tishri. During this time every year, all people are judged by God.

"L'SHANAH TOVAH TIKATEIVU"

The Talmud's idea of three books being opened on Rosh Hashanah inspired a traditional holiday greeting. It is *"L'shanah tovah tikateivu."* This is Hebrew for "May you be inscribed [in the Book of Life] for a good year." These words are appropriate to say to family and friends at home or the synagogue on Rosh Hashanah. But using the greeting after Rosh Hashanah is considered impolite. According to Jewish tradition, some sayings are only considered appropriate during certain holidays or times of year.

The Talmud contains writings, debates, and commentary from many rabbis. In some of these writings, the rabbis discuss how Rosh Hashanah should be observed.

They must pass before God as a sheep passes before a shepherd. The Talmud also describes the theme of God's judgment as part of Rosh Hashanah. In the Talmud, Jewish scholars introduced the idea that God opens three books on Rosh Hashanah. The first book is for people who are wicked. The second is for those who are good. The third is for average people, who fall

When the moon is in its new moon phase, it is blocked from view or appears as a thin crescent in the sky. This is because the side of the moon that is illuminated by the sun is facing away from Earth.

in the middle. People who fall in the middle have ten days to repent for their actions. These ten days last from Rosh Hashanah until Yom Kippur, the Day of Judgment. During these ten days, people pray, seek forgiveness from those they've wronged, and ask God not to punish them for their wrongdoing. These actions help people ensure that God will write their names in the Book of Life and allow them to live another year. If their names are written in the Book of Death, they are judged as sinners and will not live another year. On Yom Kippur, the books are closed.

A TWO-DAY CELEBRATION

In the Jewish lunar calendar, Rosh Hashanah begins when the new moon rises on the first day of Tishri. In ancient times, a group of Jewish leaders called the Sanhedrin decided when the first day began. When the new moon appeared, the Sanhedrin sent messengers to the surrounding areas to deliver the news. But it took time for messengers to reach some

PERSPECTIVES

NEW MOON

In ancient Jerusalem, the easiest way for people to tell when Rosh Hashanah started was to look for the moon in the night sky. If they couldn't see it, it was in the new moon phase. This meant that the month of Tishri and Rosh Hashanah had just started. People reported their findings to the Sanhedrin. The Sanhedrin made sure the observers' reports were accurate. Then they would declare, "New moon!" and send messengers to spread the word across the land.

regions, especially areas outside Israel. By the time the messengers reached Jews in these regions, the first day of Rosh Hashanah was already over. Because of this, the New Year celebration was allowed to continue until the end of the second day. Even after the calendar became fixed and everyone knew when Rosh Hashanah would fall, the rabbis decided to keep the custom of celebrating Rosh Hashanah for two days. This applied to people inside and outside of Israel. Today, all Jews around the world celebrate Rosh Hashanah for two days.

In the hundreds of years that followed, Jews developed many new ways of celebrating. These included prayers and blessings. Gathering with family and friends at home and at synagogues became an important part of the Jewish New Year celebration.

STRAIGHT TO THE SOURCE

The main theme of Rosh Hashanah is God's judgment of people who have sinned during the past year. In the Talmud, Rabbi Kruspedai, who lived in Israel in the 200s CE, quotes his teacher Rabbi Johanan:

> *Three books are opened on Rosh Hashanah: One for the utterly wicked, one for the wholly good, and one for the average class of people. The wholly righteous are at once inscribed, as life is decreed for them; the entirely wicked are at once inscribed, and destruction destined for them; the average class is held in the balance from Rosh Hashanah until Yom Kippur. If they prove themselves worthy they are inscribed for life, if not they are inscribed for destruction.*

Source: Elon Gilad. "Rosh Hashanah Wasn't Always the 'New Year.' Here's This Jewish Holiday's History." *Haaretz*, 5 Sept. 2021, haaretz.com. Accessed 5 Mar. 2023.

WHAT'S THE BIG IDEA?

Take a close look at this passage. What is the main connection being made between Rosh Hashanah and God's judgment? What can you tell about how Jews view their relationship with God?

מגדנית
מאפה של

CHAPTER FOUR

ROSH HASHANAH OVER TIME

Over time, Jews developed many new traditions and practices that carried special meaning for them. For example, food became an important part of celebrating Rosh Hashanah. The tradition of eating honey began around the 600s CE. This sweet food symbolizes a sweet start to the new year. Calf heads were also popular at Rosh Hashanah meals. They were thought to represent starting the year "ahead." Later, fish heads and other fish dishes replaced calf heads.

Today, many bakeries sell special round loaves of challah for Rosh Hashanah. Some loaves are flavored with raisins or honey.

Gefilte fish is often served with carrot slices and chrain, a paste made out of beets and horseradish.

Ashkenazi Jews, whose ancestors lived in Central and Eastern Europe, celebrated with gefilte fish. This is a ground-up mixture of different kinds of fish. Sephardic Jews, whose ancestors lived in Spain, Portugal, North Africa, and the Middle East, enjoyed fish dishes such as *chraime*, a spicy fish stew in tomato sauce.

By about 1000 CE, European Jews had started eating new Rosh Hashanah foods. This included challah, a braided bread made with eggs. Jews also began eating new seasonal fruits from their regions, such as apples, grapes, and pomegranates. This practice evolved into the Rosh Hashanah tradition of dipping apples in honey. Eating pomegranates became popular because of the belief that pomegranates contained 613 seeds, the same as the number of Jewish commandments.

CASTING OFF SINS

Another common Rosh Hashanah ritual is the practice of tashlik. This first became popular in the 1400s. It involves Jews emptying their pockets of bread and small food scraps and throwing them into a body of water, such as a river or sea.

In Hebrew, the word *tashlik* means

PERSPECTIVES

RABBIS AND TASHLIK

Ancient rabbis did not approve of tashlik. They felt that it cleared people of their sins too easily. In their view, Rosh Hashanah practices were supposed to be more reflective and internal rather than outwardly performed. The rabbis thought this helped people better understand where they went wrong and learn how to avoid mistakes in the future. But tashlik grew in popularity. It remains popular today. It is now seen as something to be performed along with inner reflection rather than in place of it.

SHABBAT

From sundown on Friday to sundown on Saturday, Jews observe Shabbat. This day is set aside for holiness and rest. The practice of observing Shabbat on every seventh day is commanded in the Torah. It is also discussed in later parts of the Hebrew Bible and other writings. When Rosh Hashanah falls on a Saturday, certain customs and practices must be avoided or postponed until the next day. Carrying anything on Shabbat is discouraged, so the shofar cannot be used in the synagogue. Jews cannot carry breadcrumbs to participate in tashlik on Shabbat either.

"you shall cast away." The practice is meant to symbolize casting off one's sins and broken promises. Tashlik traditionally takes place on the afternoon of the first day of Rosh Hashanah. But if the first day of Rosh Hashanah falls on Shabbat, the Jewish day of rest, tashlik is performed on the second day.

ROSH HASHANAH GREETINGS

During the 1800s, Jews began sending greeting cards to family and friends for Rosh Hashanah. These were often postcards containing short notes. One traditional

Rosh Hashanah message was *Shana tova*, or "Good year." A more religious greeting was *Gemar chatima tova*, which means "May you be well sealed [in the Book of Life]." These cards became a way to keep in touch with loved ones during the year.

Sometimes Rosh Hashanah cards also contained messages asking for forgiveness. People sent the cards to apologize to those they had hurt. This was another way to practice tashlik and mend broken relationships. Today, greeting cards are still used for this purpose.

FURTHER EVIDENCE

Chapter Four talks about Rosh Hashanah traditions and customs. What was one of the main points of this chapter? What evidence is included to support this point? Watch the video at the website below. Does the information in the video support the main point of the chapter? Does it present new evidence?

ROSH HASHANAH

abdocorelibrary.com/rosh-hashanah

שויתייהוהלנגדי
תמיד

CHAPTER FIVE

ROSH HASHANAH TODAY

Rosh Hashanah continues to be an important Jewish holiday. It is the start of a very holy time of year. Many people begin preparing for it during the Hebrew month of Elul. This is the month before Tishri.

Today, Jews celebrate Rosh Hashanah in a variety of ways. Some are traditional and formal. Others are modern and informal. Most Jews celebrate Rosh Hashanah by attending services at the synagogue and gathering with family and friends for special meals.

Rosh Hashanah and Yom Kippur services include special prayers and music that fit the holiday's themes. Attendance at these services is usually very high.

During Elul, tens of thousands of people visit Jerusalem's Western Wall for selihoth prayer services.

PREPARING FOR ROSH HASHANAH

During Elul, Jews begin the process of spiritual and personal reflection. Many read spiritual texts. They may visit the graves of family members and friends who have passed away. They take time to honor and remember them. The shofar is sounded in the synagogue every day during Elul, except on Shabbat. It serves as a wake-up call to remind Jews that the High Holidays are coming.

Elul also includes a special daily service called selihoth, which is recited at the synagogue or at home. *Selihoth* means "forgiveness" in Hebrew. At these services, Jews read prayers and poems about God's forgiveness. Ashkenazi Jews have this service late at night or in the early morning during the week before Rosh Hashanah. Sephardic Jews perform Selihoth every morning during Elul.

THE COLOR WHITE

The color white has come to represent Rosh Hashanah. During Elul, the covers of a synagogue's Torah scrolls are switched to special white ones. The white covers are used for 40 days, all the way through Yom Kippur. Some people also choose to dress in white clothing on Rosh Hashanah. The color represents purity, newness, and the idea that God makes one's sins white as snow during the Days of Awe.

CELEBRATING ROSH HASHANAH

Celebrations are held at sundown to begin the first day of Rosh Hashanah. It is customary to light candles and

The mahzor contains a collection of religious texts, songs, and prayers for both Rosh Hashanah and Yom Kippur services.

say blessings. Families attend services at the synagogue that evening and morning services on the following day. Many Jews wear new or white clothes on Rosh Hashanah to symbolize a fresh start to the year.

Synagogue services often involve reciting prayers from the mahzor, the Rosh Hashanah prayer book. Services also include readings from the Torah scrolls, which are taken out of their arks, or holding cabinets, for the occasion. The shofar is used for daytime services. It is blown about 100 times in different patterns of long and short notes. This directs attention toward prayer and inner reflection. There are morning services on the second day of Rosh Hashanah as well.

Before or after evening services, family and friends gather at one another's homes for festive dinners. They light candles and say blessings and prayers before the meal starts. The next day, they may also have a special lunch after the

PERSPECTIVES

SEDER PLATES

A seder is a ceremonial Jewish dinner that involves eating symbolic foods from a special seder plate. This practice is almost universally associated with the Jewish Passover holiday. But some Jews choose to make seder plates for Rosh Hashanah. This practice is particularly popular with Sephardic Jews, along with Mizrahi Jews from North Africa and the Middle East. A Rosh Hashanah seder plate might consist of various sweet and seasonal foods. These may include pomegranate seeds, string beans, leeks, pumpkin, carrots, fish, and apples with honey.

Public tashlik services are often held at local beaches, seashores, or riverside areas. For example, some synagogues host tashlik services at Venice Beach in California.

morning services. At Rosh Hashanah meals, the table is usually set with the best tablecloth and plates. Jews often eat apples dipped in honey and round-shaped challah to symbolize the circle of life and God's crown. No sour or bitter foods are allowed at the table.

Some Jews perform tashlik during the afternoon at an outdoor body of water. This may be a lake, river, stream, or even an ocean. People can use traditional breadcrumbs or more natural materials such as pebbles. Tashlik remains an important and meaningful tradition for many Jews.

Many old Rosh Hashanah traditions are valued and practiced throughout the world. They connect Jews to their ancient past. At the same time, new traditions continue to emerge and find their place in Rosh Hashanah celebrations. All these practices provide Jews with a powerful link to both the past and the future.

EXPLORE ONLINE

Chapter Five discusses how the Rosh Hashanah ritual of tashlik is practiced today. A variety of different materials can be used for tashlik. The article at the website below offers some examples. How are these materials similar to those mentioned in Chapter Five? How are they different? What new information did you learn from the article?

HOW TO CAST AWAY YOUR SINS AND PROTECT THE ENVIRONMENT

abdocorelibrary.com/rosh-hashanah

IMPORTANT DATES

597 BCE
The Babylonians invade Israel. They destroy the Holy Temple in Jerusalem and force Jewish people into exile.

592–570
The Hebrew prophet Ezekiel first uses the name Rosh Hashanah in his writings.

538
Many Jews return to Israel from Babylonia. They begin celebrating Rosh Hashanah as a New Year holiday.

458
Ezra the Scribe returns to Jerusalem and reorganizes Jewish life. He speaks about the purpose of Rosh Hashanah.

70 CE
The Romans destroy the Second Temple in Jerusalem.

220
The Mishnah is completed. It discusses Rosh Hashanah.

220–600s
The Talmud is written. It mentions Rosh Hashanah practices.

600s
Jews begin eating symbolic foods during Rosh Hashanah.

1000s
European Jews begin the tradition of eating challah and seasonal fruit during Rosh Hashanah.

1400s
Jews popularize the tashlik during Rosh Hashanah.

1800s
Jews begin sending Rosh Hashanah greeting cards.

STOP AND THINK

Say What?

Studying the history of holidays can mean learning a lot of new vocabulary. Find five words in this book you've never heard before. Use a dictionary to find out what they mean. Then write the meanings in your own words and use each word in a new sentence.

Surprise Me

Chapter Four discusses Rosh Hashanah traditions. After reading this book, what two or three facts about these traditions did you find most surprising? Write a few sentences about each fact. Why did you find each fact surprising?

You Are There

This book discusses Rosh Hashanah services. Imagine you are attending a Rosh Hashanah service. Write a journal entry about your experience. What did you observe? What did you think about? Be sure to add plenty of detail to your notes.

Another View

This book talks about Babylonia's influence on Rosh Hashanah. As you know, every source is different. Ask a librarian or another adult to help you find another source about this topic. Write a short essay comparing and contrasting the new source's point of view with that of this book's author. What is the point of view of each author? How are they similar and why? How are they different and why?

GLOSSARY

cantor
a person who leads songs and prayers during a synagogue service

custom
a widely accepted way of doing something, specific to a group

prophet
a person who receives and relays a message believed to be from God

rabbi
a Jewish religious leader and teacher

rabbinic
relating to rabbis or Jewish law or teachings

repentance
the act of expressing sincere regret for one's actions

ritual
a set of actions regularly performed in a certain order

symbolic
representing something important

synagogue
a place where Jews gather to pray, worship, and study together

temple
the House of God in Jerusalem, where prayers were said and sacrifices were made

ONLINE RESOURCES

To learn more about Rosh Hashanah, visit our free resource websites below.

Visit **abdocorelibrary.com** or scan this QR code for free Common Core resources for teachers and students, including vetted activities, multimedia, and booklinks, for deeper subject comprehension.

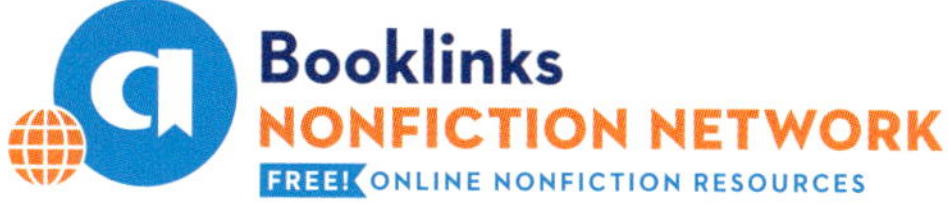

Visit **abdobooklinks.com** or scan this QR code for free additional online weblinks for further learning. These links are routinely monitored and updated to provide the most current information available.

LEARN MORE

Havemeyer, Janie. *A Look at Judaism*. BrightPoint Press, 2024.

Pinson, Rochie. *The KIDS Book of Challah*. Feldheim Publishers, 2022.

INDEX

About the Author

Hilary Margitich writes and reviews fiction and nonfiction children's books. She is a graduate student in children's literature curriculum and instruction at Penn State University and holds master's degrees from Cornell University. She lives in the Boston, Massachusetts, area with her husband and three children. She enjoys researching and writing about history, religion, and culture.